❧ *I'll Come Back in the Springtime*

I'll Come Back
in the Springtime

John F. Kennedy and the Irish

BY MAURICE N. HENNESSY

IVES WASHBURN, INC. • NEW YORK

I'll Come Back in the Springtime

Author's Note

❧ ON January 12, 1957, Senator John F. Kennedy was guest of honor of the Irish Institute at the Hotel Commodore, New York City. In introducing him, Paul O'Dwyer, President of the Institute, said:

"Our legislative halls are generally divided into two groups: those who feel the public need is best served by favoring the entrenched interests who, they say, can be expected to care for the less fortunate citizen in one form or another; and those committed to the principle that it is the obligation of government to serve the needs of our citizens and end inequities among them. Our guest has taken a leadership position among the latter forces. It is because of his humane and enlightened approach to the problems of our times that we sought him to be our honored guest. . . .

In his address that evening Senator Kennedy said:

"All of us of Irish descent are bound together by the ties that come from a common experience; experience which may exist only in memories and in legend, but which is real enough to those who possess it. And thus whether we live in Cork or in Boston, in New York or in Sydney, we are all members of a great family which is

v

linked together by that strongest of chains—a common past. It is strange to think that the wellspring from which this great fraternal empire has sprung is but a small island in the far Atlantic with a population only a fraction of the size of this Empire State. But this is the source, and it is this green and misty island to the east that we honor here tonight—honoring it particularly, I have in mind, for its devotion to human liberty.

"I do not maintain that the Irish were the only race to display extraordinary devotion to liberty, or the only people to struggle unceasingly for their national independence. History proves otherwise. But the special contribution of the Irish, I believe—the emerald thread that runs throughout the tapestry of their past—has been the constancy, the endurance, the faith that they displayed through endless centuries of foreign oppression—centuries in which even the most rudimentary religious and civil rights were denied to them—centuries in which their mass destruction by poverty, disease and starvation were ignored by their conquerors. . . .

"Let us here tonight resolve that our nation will forever hold out its hands to those who struggle for freedom today, as Ireland struggled for a thousand years. We will not leave them to be 'sheep without a shepherd when the snow shuts out the sky.' Instead we will recognize that whether a man be Hungarian or Irish, Catholic or Jew, white or black, there forever burns within his breast the unquenchable desire to be free."

Perhaps it was with this occasion in mind that about a year ago Mr. O'Dwyer approached me with the suggestion that I write a book about the late President John F. Kennedy which would not only emphasize his Irish background, his love of Ireland, and his association with its people, but also throw some light on how and why he differed from the familiar Irish-American political figure of an earlier day. As an Irishman who now lives in the United States, the idea appealed to me enormously, and I began my research by visiting as many as possible of the people in Ireland that Kennedy had seen.

This Irish journey was made easy by a friend of many years, Hector Legge, editor of the Dublin *Sunday Independent*. I am deeply grateful for his help. I am also grateful to A. M. Sullivan, historian of the American-Irish Historical Society, for valuable advice and assistance.

Maurice N. Hennessy

New York
June, 1966

Contents

ix

Introduction

🍀 JOHN KENNEDY loved Ireland and the Irish people. He studied the history of his forefathers and was filled with that strange mixture of nostalgia, pride, and vicarious Irish patriotism which is characteristic of so many of Irish heritage who find themselves far from Ireland.

The wave of emotion that grew through four summer days in Ireland in 1963 reached its climax as the President boarded the plane for his return to the United States. He said, "I certainly will come back in the springtime," and probably meant it, but the fact that he did not live long enough to carry out his promise gave the words special poignancy for the Irish. They symbolized that tragic quality which has always been a part of Irish history.

The whole Irish visit was filled with incidents which indicated his deep love for the country and the people. On one occasion he said: "This is not the land of my birth, but it is the land for which I hold the greatest affection." One of the more intriguing aspects of Kennedy's official visit to Ireland was the informality of his remarks about his love for his own heritage and Ireland. "I can imagine nothing more pleasant than continuing day after day to drive through the streets of Dublin. . . . I may come back and do it."

When John Kennedy addressed the Irish Parliament he made another memorable statement: "I am deeply honored to be your guest in the Free Parliament of a Free Ireland. If this nation had achieved its present political and economic stature a century or so ago, my great-grandfather might never have left New Ross, and I might, *if fortunate,* be sitting down there with you." This was not the language of diplomacy, nor was it prompted by the hope of any political advantage. There were those who believed that John Kennedy's official visit to Ireland was a vote-catching one. This was not true; too many Irishmen in America were anxious to dissociate themselves from Ireland, and particularly from the American politicians of Irish descent. In fact, after the 1960 Presidential election, Kennedy told many of his friends that he obtained only about fifty percent of the Irish vote.

Although the official Irish visit was for Kennedy the highlight of his relations with Ireland, long before he became President his ties with the country were strong.

Frequently he referred in conversation to the early greatness of Ireland, to its heroes, sung and unsung. He believed with Æ (George William Russell) that: "An aristocracy of lordly and chivalrous heroes is bound in time to create a great democracy by the reflection of their character in the mass, and the idea of the divine right of the people. If this sequence cannot be traced in any one respect with historical regularity, it is because of the complexity of national life, its varied needs, the vicissitudes of history, and its infinite change of sentiment."

It is indicative of his feelings for the Irish people that on the night of his nomination as the Democratic Presidential candidate in San Francisco, he sent a special message to them. He found time to send another message to the Irish people on the night of his inauguration: "I wanted to take this opportunity to send my greetings to Ireland; we also think of Ireland as the Standard Bearer. We fight the good fight."

John F. Kennedy's Irish heritage and his ties with Ireland and its people are of interest not only to Americans of Irish descent and to citizens of Ireland, but to anyone who wants to know more about the influences that shaped the man and made him what he was.

🍀 *I'll Come Back in the Springtime*

1

Irish Ancestry

❧ JOHN KENNEDY'S ANCESTORS first
came to prominence in Ireland in the 11th century
when Brian Boru, whose name was O'Kenedy, de-
stroyed the power of the Norsemen at the Battle of
Clontarf. On the occasion of the President's visit to
Ireland the Chief Herald of the Genealogical Office
of Ireland prepared a grant of a coat of arms for him;
it was based on his family history and his position as
the Chief Executive of the United States.

In his first State of the Union message delivered
to Congress on January 30th, 1961, the President
used these words: "On the Presidential coat of arms,
the American eagle holds in his right talon the olive
branch, while in his left is held a bundle of arrows.
We intend to give equal attention to both." The
Chief Herald gave particular attention to this statement when preparing the O'Kenedy coat of arms—
Ireland's special gift to him. The crest of the coat of

1

arms has an armed hand holding a sheaf of arrows between two olive branches, echoing in a general way the
similar device on the arms of the United States and
playing on the theme of the State of the Union message. The most prominent theme in this coat of arms
is the traditional or "basic" arms of the O'Kenedys
of Ormonde. Noteworthy are the famous three helmets, which in this design have been slightly modified
by changing them from their natural color to gold.

The three helmets on the O'Kenedy arms are taken
to refer to the three prominent septs within the clan,
which were distinguished by words referring to the
color of their hair, viz.: Ó Cinnéide *fionn* (fair),
Ó Cinnéide *donn* (brown) and Ó Cinnéide *ruadh*
(red).

The coat of arms of these O'Kenedys is distinguished from that of President Kennedy and his immediate family by the introduction in the latter of a
recollection of Fitzgerald of Desmond representing
his maternal grandfather's side. This takes the form
of a border on the shield so divided as to suggest the
Fitzgerald saltire or red St. Andrew's cross backing
the Kennedy shield.

No motto is included in the coat of arms as it was
considered that a choice of so personal a matter as
the motto should be left to President Kennedy himself.

The presentation of the coat of arms to President
Kennedy was made by Dr. T. J. Kiernan, Irish Am-

bassador in Washington, at a ceremony held in the White House on St. Patrick's Day, 1961.

In order to bring the story of his early ancestors closer to him, an original vellum deed of treaty concluded in 1336 between the Earl of Ormonde and O'Kenedy, who was then Chief of the O'Kenedy clan, was given to him. The document is in Latin, and has affixed to it by ribbon the seal of O'Kenedy; the Earl of Ormonde's seal is missing.

The Ormondes later became the avowed enemies of the Fitzgeralds; the two houses caused considerable bloodshed during the 15th and 16th centuries.

Brian Boru was chief of the O'Kenedy clan and King of Munster, the southern province of Ireland. The O'Kenedy seat was the Rock of Cashel—the place where Saint Patrick is reputed to have used the shamrock to illustrate the Christian belief in the Trinity, One God in Three Divine Persons. The symbol of the shamrock in the 5th century meant much to Europe, for St. Patrick established a college and a university in the city of Armagh with such remarkable scholarship that they were famous all over the Continent.

After the Battle of Clontarf, Brian "The O'Kenedy" was crowned king not only of his own Province of Munster but of all of Ireland. The definite article "The" was the proudest title that any member of a family could bear; it signified that its user held the very highest possible rank in the family.

During the period of his glory, Brian Boru, the

valiant prince O'Kenedy, defeated his enemies in fourteen pitched battles, and although Brian himself was killed at Clontarf, his armies were victorious and succeeded in destroying the power of the Vikings in Ireland forever.

After the death of Brian, the O'Kenedy clan began to lose its power. However, their love of country was

OPPOSITE: *The Kennedy Coat of Arms: Prepared as a special grant to John F. Kennedy from the Irish Government and presented with warmest friendship to the President on St. Patrick's Day of 1961, his first year in office.*

In Ireland, during his visit while President, another gift was a vellum deed of the treaty concluded in 1336 between the Earl of Ormonde and O'Kenedy—a Kennedy forebear.

proved by the number of Irish soldiers named Kenedy who served in the ranks of Irish armies and fought in many battles.

The 1798 Irish revolt had its origin in County Wexford, the birthplace of John Kennedy's immediate ancestors, and it was one of the chapters of Irish history with which the President was most familiar. A number of his ancestors took part in the Rising and lost their lives. Two of his great-granduncles fought at the Battle of Ross until one of them fell after being struck by three bullets. The second uncle disengaged himself from the battle and carried his wounded brother to the river trying to escape to the family farm at Dunganstown. He succeeded in reaching a gate near the house, but fell exhausted when he tried to open it. To this day the gate is known as "Three Bullet Gate."

On President Kennedy's maternal side there was also rich Irish tradition. While none of its members achieved the national status of Brian Boru, nonetheless it had established many records of great courage and patriotism. Also it had certain unique qualities about it. The Fitzgeralds were descendants of the Anglo-Normans who settled in Ireland at the instigation of the English. Their purpose was to anglicize Ireland, but to the dismay of the English, they became "more Irish than the Irish themselves." They were known as the "Geraldines," and so complete was their conversion to Irish tradition and custom that they achieved European renown for the fervor of their Irish patriotism.

In the reign of Henry VIII of England, as well as for a long time previously, the Geraldine family comprised two great branches of which the Earl of Desmond and the Earl of Kildare were the respective heads, the latter the paramount one and the ancestor of President Kennedy's mother.

The Kennedys and the Fitzgeralds left Ireland, roughly at about the same time, in the late 1840s. John F. Kennedy's great-grandfather came in 1849; he landed on Noddle's Island in East Boston and found work as a cooper. At the time, he was 26 years old and in very poor health. Shortly after arriving in America, he married Bridget Murphy. In 1858 his only son, Patrick, John F. Kennedy's grandfather, was born, ten months before his own death. He had three older daughters.

Bridget Kennedy's struggle to rear four children is a depressing story. At one time she opened a small store where she sold odds and ends and stationery. Pat helped in the store when he was old enough. Later his mother became a hairdresser. Pat grew up in a family that was poor in the world's gifts, but rich in love and human warmth. As a youth he worked as a stevedore and longshoreman and, as the years went by, like so many of his colleagues he became involved in politics. Later he married and had a son, deciding to call him Joseph Patrick, simply because there had been two Patrick Josephs in the family already and he wished to avoid confusion. From the docks he graduated to the ownership of a saloon in Boston. This enabled him to keep in closer touch with political happenings in the city.

In the meantime Thomas Fitzgerald, John F. Kennedy's great-grandfather, who, like Pat Kennedy, had also come from County Wexford, was earning $6 a month as a farm laborer in South Acton, Massachusetts. On this amount he tried to support seven sons, the third of whom was John Francis Fitzgerald, later to be known as "Honey Fitz." Like Pat Kennedy, Thomas Fitzgerald also managed to graduate to a store. This one was a grocery and liquor store and it provided an environment in which Honey Fitz managed to thrive. He had a rough boyhood; in his own words, "My playgrounds were the streets and wharves with busy ships from every port of the world."

By the end of the nineteenth century, John F. Kennedy's maternal grandfather had become a power in the political life of Boston. It was at a time when the Brahmins of Boston were losing control of the political machine to the Irish. Meanwhile, John F. Fitzgerald (Honey Fitz) had married Josephine Hannon.

Johnny Fitz was two years older than thirteen-year-old Mary Josephine Hannon when he first met her. The meeting place was her mother's kitchen, where she was washing dishes when she heard the greeting "Hello, there!" The peaches-and-cream, brown-haired, slender young woman turned and smiled at the young man who was later to become her husband. Turning away from him, she left the kitchen and went upstairs. Young Miss Hannon was terribly shy. During following weeks, despite repeated visits to the Hannon home, Johnny could do little to break through the girl's diffidence.

John F. Fitzgerald didn't give up. When he encountered Mary Hannon anywhere in the neighborhood he persisted in his efforts to win her attention. Then, some years later, Johnny picked twelve barrels of apples in one day—a feat that impressed not only the local farmers but Mary Hannon, who saw it as proof that her suitor was both hard-working and ambitious. After this incident the young couple saw each other more frequently and married not long afterward.

John was twenty-six years old and Mary was twenty-four at the time they married and began their life together.

Johnny Fitz was doing well in the insurance business, for he had the kind of blarney a successful insurance salesman needs, and so many friends he could always find a number who needed insurance protection. An East Boston neighbor of P. J. Kennedy, who insured his stable with Johnny Fitz, remembers how barren Fitzgerald's office was.

"There was a battered desk" in the tiny office, "and not one chair," he recalled.

John Kennedy's great-grandfathers brought a strong belief in Irish tradition with them to Boston.

The Irish immigrants who flocked to Boston during the last century came to find work and escape the specter of hunger, which was such a part of their lives in Ireland. In addition to the desire for these advantages in America, they also brought a traditional attitude toward the rule of law other than the Church, an attitude that still exists in Ireland.

So innate a part of the Irish character did this aversion to law become that when the Irish Free State was established in 1922, one of the major problems facing the government was to give the people a sense of legal obligation, especially in financial matters.

To counteract this negative side of Irish tradition, there were distinct advantages in Irish training, especially where family loyalty and national affairs were concerned. The ties in the home, strengthened by conscientious parents, the belief that patriotism was a virtue next to religion, and the firm conviction that Christianity was the world's most potent force were all a definite part of Irish upbringing.

But much had happened since his great-grandfathers' time. The weakness in the Irish character and Boston Brahmin resentment had built up a barrier against the Irish and had created an aura of dislike and disrespect which is still evident. There was an easily recognizable reason for this. The people the Irish immigrants met in Boston were the descendants of the English who based their thinking about the Irish on the reports from English newspapers. They considered the Irish as a group of dissidents, ignorant, inartistic, and far removed from any potential greatness. They were almost totally ignorant of Ireland's past cultural richness, and the few who had any knowledge of it considered it an accident of history best forgotten.

As a young boy in Boston, Kennedy knew much of two things: the Ireland of his grandfathers, and Boston politics. There was always ample opportunity for him to assimilate the romantic and often exaggerated tales about the former. His grandfathers were also a wonderful source of training for a political career, for they had been thoroughly immersed in politics themselves. Honey Fitz was an adroit politician who knew the highways and byways that led to political success. Patrick Kennedy, the successful bar owner in Boston, learned all the angles for establishing oneself in a position of power where one can influence others. It was from the paternal ancestor, rather than the maternal, that Kennedy learned to understand Ireland and the Irish character, for Pat Kennedy was an Irish patriot. And as he grew up he came to realize that there was an intellectual potential in the Irish that could be harnessed if the native qualities of the true Celt were exploited. So at an early age John Kennedy became one of that small minority of Irish-Americans who live with the true intellectual richness of Ireland, who can be *of* the political world but who can also raise themselves above it.

2

Politics

🍀 WHEN AS A YOUNG NOVICE in the political game John F. Kennedy decided to run for the Eleventh Massachusetts Congressional District in Boston, he was in effect out to prove that there was a third class of Irish. The seasoned Irish politicians in the city looked upon his candidacy as an impertinence and were loud in their declaration that a brash young Harvard man, scion of a very wealthy family, was playing at politics. The "shanty," as well as the "lace curtain," Irish were in little sympathy with the fledgling. They believed that he did not understand the deep-rooted dislike of the Irish politicians in Boston; they were convinced that anyone of Irish heritage who was foolhardy enough to operate independently, without the Irish political juggernaut to clear the path to victory, was doomed to failure. The truth, of course, was that they failed to realize that John Kennedy had discovered for himself that there was a change in the wind and that the oratorical, exaggerative, and flamboyant era of Boston politics was doomed. He had tasted the spicy, fresh tang of intellectualism and believed firmly that this was a superior goal to strive for in politics. Although he was only a neophyte, the success of his book *While England Slept* and the vast amount of knowledge he had assimilated while writing it gave an added fillip to his belief that he was on the threshold of a new political era. At any rate, he believed enough to stake a career on it.

And Kennedy knew full well that in Boston much of the prejudice against the Irish still remained. He realized that his father's appointment as Ambassador to the Court of St. James's had been an insult to the Brahmins of Boston and would not be easily forgotten. Finally, he saw that as far as Boston was concerned, youth and political office were an untried and thus far unacceptable mixture. On the other hand, because he believed that rationality is superior to sentimental Irish nostalgia, Celtic braggadocio, and oratorical harlotry, he was convinced that the time was ripe for his kind of politics.

Kennedy was, of course, right. He saw in Boston an opportunity to prove that in America one could triumph over the dire predictions of the pundits and win a political victory. And so as Professor Burns * wrote: "Boston thought it had seen everything in politics, but here was something new. Kennedy was

* See footnote, p. 19.

only twenty-eight years old. Still yellow from the Atabrine he had taken to fight malaria, reserved, gaunt, almost emaciated-looking, he was a polar opposite to the familiar image of the derby-hatted, loud-talking, paunchy Boston politician. Many of the latter did not take the young candidate very seriously. He would get a bad case of burned fingers, they told one another; Boston politics was for big boys. Wait till the pros got into the race."

Although he was not committed ideologically in the sense that the old stagers were, young Kennedy had his own Democratic ideals. He saw a new America destined to take over the leadership of the world in international affairs. He was aware that the isolationism and narrowness of many of the experienced professional politicians had to go. He was convinced that instead of relating the world to the United States, the time was coming when, despite its vast wealth and power, the United States would have to start relating itself to the world. In the very newness of this conception John Kennedy realized that his political organization had to come from young men and not from the older professionals. So he searched amongst his college friends and associates and picked what was really the nucleus of the "Irish Mafia."

It was in the selection of this group of young men that Kennedy displayed his deep respect for Irish innate ability. Aware as he was of the deeply-rooted prejudice against the Irish in Boston and fully conscious of the Irish politicians' reputation for dishonesty, he could have been expected to seek aides from amongst another group. Also, the Harvard young men of his choice were inclined to be liberals, a further difficulty in an age and place where young liberals were intellectually suspect. But John Kennedy had faith in people; his respect for the "Animal rationale" was profound, and, as events proved, it was justified.

John Kennedy's success in the Congressional election spurred his ambition. One writer said of him: "He was candid in his aspiration for the presidency and was willing to give all that he possessed in mind and body toward that end. It brings back the incident of the Gridiron Dinner of 1958 when the Washington correspondents of the nation's leading papers lampooned him in a skit which depicted a young lad from Boston caught in his Fauntleroy pants, trying to climb the spiked fence of the White House lawn. J.F.K. enjoyed the joke at his expense and then rose to make a statement in rebuttal. He admitted that the White House had its attraction for him as an ambitious legislator, and asked permission to read a telegram from his father which purported to say in effect, 'My son, news has come to me of your aspirations to be president of the United States, a worthy ambition for any young American. I want you to know that I approve your aim in life and will support

your efforts toward this end with all of the resources
at my command. However, let me add that while I
am willing to pay for your election, I will not pay
for a landslide.' The telegram was as prophetic as it
was apocryphal."

But commensurate with his ambition and purpose
was his great common sense. He was fully aware that
despite his first and important victory, he was a mere
tyro in politics and that the period as Congressman
was to be one of initiation and instruction. His Massachusetts victory could not be considered a triumph
for Ireland; in the eyes of most Republicans it was
just another politician's success. And that was just
what he did not wish it to be considered, especially
since he attributed his election to his own unique
approach to postwar politics.

John Kennedy did just what he intended to do
during his tenure as Congressman: he learned the
ropes within the administration itself; he studied the
psychology of his colleagues and prepared himself
mentally for the next rung of the ladder.

As Kennedy grew in political experience and
looked ahead to the White House, he saw clearly
some of the pitfalls before him. As a Catholic Irishman he realized fully that beneath the fundamental
belief in religious liberty there did exist in the
United States a barrier against a Catholic President.
The memory of the fate of Al Smith was always with
him.

While Kennedy never ceased to learn as a Congressman, the assimilative process did not prevent his voicing definite opinions about much needed legislation. In fact, his youthful enthusiasm and intrepid approach on some issues startled many of the older members who looked on him as a brash, green, Irish politician with unorthodox and liberal ideas—one who posed many problems for the die-hards. A scion of a wealthy family, he was most vociferous on the subject of subsidized housing for the poor; he was the enemy of slum landlords. Although a member of the American Legion and of the Veterans of Foreign Wars, he had the courage to say, "The leadership of the American Legion has not had a constructive thought for the benefit of this country since 1918." In February of 1951, while testifying before a Senate committee on the issue of sending troops to Europe, his opinion differed from that of his father. His answer to Senator Walter George on that occasion also demonstrated a sense of diplomacy: "That is my position; I think you should ask my father directly as to his position."

After six years as a Congressman, Kennedy began to look to the horizon, and in 1952 he decided to oppose Henry Cabot Lodge, Jr., for the office of United States Senator from Massachusetts. The reaction to this announcement was exactly the same as when he declared his intention to run for Congress in 1946. The political experts rated his chance of success as almost nil; his friends were aghast at what they considered his undue political audacity, while many of the rank and file among the voters considered him merely a young Irish politician in a hurry. James MacGregor Burns, author of *John Kennedy: A Political Profile,* summed it up admirably when he wrote: "Rarely in American politics have hunter and quarry so resembled each other. Not only were they both tall, young, handsome, and winning, each a Brahmin in his own way, but their careers were remarkably parallel. Like Kennedy, Lodge was a Harvard man who had had a fling at newspaper work before entering politics at an early age. Both possessed noted isolationist forebears; Lodge's grandfather, of the same name, had led the opposition to spike Woodrow Wilson's efforts to bring America into the League of Nations. Both Kennedy and Lodge could boast of their war records. Both had a reputation for appealing to the 'women's vote.' Of the two, Lodge was more suave, polished, and mature, Kennedy more tense, detached, and boyish, but each could be cool and stiff under pressure." *

The two contestants fought the battle as individuals on a high plane. The mudslinging and what scurrilous references there were came from the party

* From JOHN KENNEDY: A POLITICAL PROFILE by James MacGregor Burns. Reprinted by permission of Harcourt, Brace & World, Inc.

political machines, which had ample issues to exploit. Democrats generally opposed McCarthyism; the Republicans, on the other hand, refused to denigrate the Wisconsin witch-hunter. Lodge's friends, the stalwart old Brahmins of New England, pointed at the Irish immigrants and their political record.. Measured against high ethical standards, it was a bad one, a success story won at the price of age-old principles sacrificed for power and money.

Kennedy had another problem, the growing antipathy to Catholicism in many areas. This was due in part to the sensitive issue of federal aid to private and particularly Catholic schools. One prominent Freemason declared in 1947 that the Roman Catholic Church was determined "to destroy our liberties and further expand their theocracy as a world government." He further alleged that Catholic schools were instilling a dual allegiance in the minds of children: to the Pope first, and then to the State. Kennedy answered him by denying that American Catholics were legal subjects of the Pope. Although wishing to avoid a religious battle, he denounced the attack and refuted its reasoning.

No sooner had he declared his intention of seeking election to the Senate than the Kennedy family rallied around him, not merely to present a unified picture to the electorate, but because they were genuinely anxious to send Jack to the Senate. The Kennedy women in particular did much to further his campaign. By arranging special tea parties and coffee sessions for all and sundry, they demonstrated that the crooked-little-finger lace-curtain Irish tea parties were dignified social gatherings designed to give the guests an opportunity to meet and hear the young candidate. They were eminently successful; Kennedy defeated the deeply entrenched incumbent and once again demonstrated that he had become a really vital force in American politics.

In the next years, although facing opposition from fellow Democrats in Massachusetts, because he opposed the release of James M. Curley from prison and opposed the appointment of Michael Burke as chairman of the State Democratic Committee, Kennedy rose rapidly on the national scene.

By a very narrow margin he was defeated for the Vice Presidential nomination in 1956, but in his defeat he was again the courageous, courteous Kennedy the people began to know. As Professor Burns wrote: "Despite his grin, Kennedy looked wilted and disappointed. Yet, as things turned out, this was his great moment—the moment when he passed through a kind of political sound barrier to register on the nation's memory. The dramatic race had glued millions to their television sets. Kennedy's near-victory and sudden loss, the impression he gave of a clean-cut boy who had done his best and who was accepting defeat with a smile—all this struck at people's hearts in living rooms across the nation. In this moment of triumphant defeat, his campaign for the presidency was born." *

The years between 1956 and 1960 were rewarding ones for Kennedy. He became a national figure. He wrote for many of the more effective journals; he was vociferous on international affairs; he took a firm stand on civil rights; and he demonstrated that despite his comparative youth, he was one of the finest political brains in the country. He ran for the Senate again in 1958 and was returned unopposed. It was evident that not only was he Presidential material, but he was galloping toward the White House.

When it became apparent that Kennedy was a likely Presidential candidate, Ireland seized on the possibility and grew giddy with the notion of an Irish descendant becoming the first Catholic President of the United States. It is to the credit of the Irish that their first reaction was not: what will this do for Ireland? Rather, they took intense pride in the idea that one of their own might make it. The Irish idea had also spread to areas of the United States where there were large contingents of Irish Americans. Many of these believed that a Catholic President of Irish descent would surely smooth the path for them. Their ideas were usually nebulous but they certainly hoped.

Although Kennedy's rise had given the word "Irish" a new meaning in Eastern politics, it had in no way

* Ibid.

mitigated the strong feeling against the word "Catholic" used as a prefix for President of the United States.
Uppermost in the minds of many was the idea that a
Catholic President might find himself in a position
where his loyalty to the State would conflict with the
law of the Church. Questioned on this contingency
by a reporter, Kennedy had answered: "I can't think
of any issue where such a conflict might arise. But
suppose it did? Nobody in my church gives me orders.
It doesn't work that way. I've been in Congress for
ten years, and it has never happened. People are
afraid that Catholics take orders from a higher organization. They don't. Or at least I don't.

"Besides, I can't act as a private individual does;
my responsibility is to my constituents and to the
Constitution. So if it came to a conflict between the
two, and not just a personal moral issue, I am bound
to act for the interests of the many." Despite this
statement, doubt remained in the minds of many.
Most politicians recognized that Ireland had been the
breeding place of American Catholicism and that
there was almost a fanatical quality about many Irish
Catholics. The issue of Church and State was also
very much in debate, and many people were convinced that a Catholic President could not permit the
separation of the two.

Even among Kennedy's ardent supporters the issue
was obviously giving rise to many questions. Eleanor
Roosevelt, when asked whether she was against the

idea of a Catholic President, replied: "I did not say I was not for Kennedy; what I said was that I hoped that the first president who was elected and who was a Roman Catholic would be one whom we felt certain had the character to separate church and state completely, and I have been simply worried because I had not been sure that Senator Kennedy could do that . . . I think it will depend on the feeling that people have about the character of the man, his own qualifications. If I approved of a candidate, I would have no qualms about him because of his religion . . . I do not think a Catholic would be a handicap on the ticket."

Kennedy himself, realizing that his political opponents were certain to make a major issue of the matter, made a further statement to a *Look* reporter: "Whatever one's religion in his private life may be," he told Knebel, "for the officeholder nothing takes precedence over his oath to uphold the Constitution —including the First Amendment and the strict separation of church and state. Without reference to the presidency, I believe as a senator that the separation of church and state is fundamental to our American concept and heritage and should remain so.

"I am flatly opposed to appointment of an ambassador to the Vatican," Kennedy went on. "Whatever advantages it might have in Rome—and I'm not convinced of these—they would be more than offset by the divisive effect at home.

"The First Amendment to the Constitution is an infinitely wise one. There can be no question of a Federal Government's extending support to sustain any church or its schools. As for such fringe matters as buses, lunches, and other services, the issue is primarily social and economic and not religious. Each case must be judged on its merits within the law as *interpreted by the courts."*

The effect of this statement was surprising, for it brought forth the sharpest criticism from the Catholic press. The foremost Catholic weekly in the United States, the Jesuit *America,* attacked the Senator fiercely, declaring: "Mr. Kennedy doesn't really believe that. No religious man, be he Catholic, Protestant or Jew, holds such an opinion. A man's conscience has a bearing on his public as well as his private life."

There was also another reaction: many Catholics believed that a Catholic President would bend over backwards in order to show that he was not protecting Catholic interests. They believed that they would be better off with someone who could take a more objective view.

Strangely enough, the majority of Irish Catholics at home had little idea of what went on in religious circles in the United States. As far as they knew, Catholic procedure was little different there than it was in "Holy Ireland." They also believed that every Catholic and everyone of Irish descent would vote for their adopted son. And how they adopted him! During the political struggle for the Democratic nomination, and afterwards for the Presidency, they followed "our own boy" with intense interest. The press coverage was more than adequate, and many prayers were offered for his success which, when it came, was greeted with a "hurrah!" that was deafening and honest.

3

Visits to Ireland

✤ JOHN KENNEDY made four visits to Ireland. His first was in 1938 when his father was Ambassador to the Court of St. James's. Although he was only 21, his interest in Ireland was already strong. For a number of years he had been trying to persuade his father to take him to Ireland. Then in 1938, when the National University of Ireland decided to confer an Honorary Degree on Joseph Kennedy, the Ambassador made the occasion an excuse for the family visit. For the trip from London he hired a de Havilland 86, one of the three planes owned by what is now Ireland's National Airline, Aer Lingus.

Mr. Maher, the manager of the Dublin Airport at the time, recalls vividly the arrival of the fourteen-seater machine, for out of it stepped twelve Kennedys. "I remember them well. I remember them as the happiest and most handsome family I have ever seen."

The Kennedy family was entertained at the American Embassy in Dublin and went on a tour of Dublin and its environs, but there is no other record of any activity in Ireland on that occasion. They remained only one day and returned to London in the evening.

His second visit was more prolonged and was arranged entirely by himself. In 1947, as a young Congressman, he visited Lismore Castle near the town of Fermoy. Kennedy's love of history must have received a very strong fillip on this occasion for few places in Ireland are so steeped in it. The castle where he stayed was built by King John in the 12th century; it was the home of the Dukes of Devonshire, one of the oldest families in England, and was erected on the banks of the Blackwater River, where so many of England's literary and historic personages had made their homes.

John Kennedy's sister Kathleen was the widowed Marchioness of Hartington and the daughter-in-law of the Duke of Devonshire, hence, the reason for Kennedy's being a guest in the castle. As an avid reader of history, the young Congressman, then only 30, knew that at one time Sir Walter Raleigh had lived in the castle and that in the town of Youghal, some 15 miles away, he had planted the first potatoes and smoked the first pipe of tobacco to be used in Europe. The site of the potato planting and the very seat where Raleigh smoked the pipe are still preserved in a residence in Youghal called "Myrtle Grove." The old town has many pictures of a servant throwing water on Raleigh in the belief that he was on fire because the smoke was issuing from his mouth.

Nearby Inchiquin Castle had other memories. Later it became the home of one of the most hateful tyrants in Irish history, known as "Bloody Inchiquin." His *modus operandi* was to invite prominent Irishmen to the castle as house guests and have them murdered during the night. It had also housed the Countess of Desmond, who lived to 137. When she was over 80 she climbed an apple tree, fell out of it, and broke her hip. She recovered to live another 50 years and become one of the world's most colorful women.

It was from this lush, beautiful, and historic countryside that Kennedy set out to find the old homestead from which his great-grandfather had emigrated during the famine. When he set forth he was accompanied by Mrs. Randolph Churchill who, with Anthony Eden and various other important political personages, was also staying at the castle. He had some difficulty finding the original Kennedy home and was, at first, directed to the home of Jim Kennedy. The house stands on the banks of the River Barrow. Jim and the President's father were second cousins and the former still remembers vividly the young Congressman's visit: "He was a nice slip of a lad, but he looked very young to be a Congressman."

Jim Kennedy took the young man to the home of Mary Ryan in Dunganstown, whose grandfather in 1850 became the first Kennedy to emigrate to America. Young Kennedy was a warm and interested guest. He drank tea in the kitchen sitting by the fire and asked innumerable questions about his fore-fathers. He took pictures of the Ryan family, and when he returned to the United States sent copies back to the family. Many years later when he saw the family again on the Presidential visit, he remembered to ask Jim Kennedy whether he had received the photographs.

The Ryan homestead was a poor one. Lismore Castle, one of the most luxurious in Ireland, was a far cry from Mary Ryan's kitchen in Dunganstown, but the Congressman, commenting on the visit, said: "I spent about an hour there surrounded by chickens and pigs, and left in a flow of nostalgia and sentiment. This was punctured by the English lady turning to me as we drove off and saying, 'That was just like Tobacco Road!' She had not understood at all the magic of the afternoon."

In 1957 he went to Poland accompanied by his wife. He was a Senator at the time, and his mission was entirely one of political study. On his way back he stopped off in Dublin to pay his third visit and registered at the Shelburne Hotel, where many a United States Senator has been extended hospitality. The staff at the hotel would have had little cause to remember him then but for the fact that he was on crutches. Apparently, his back injury was giving him serious trouble at the time.

On his arrival in Dublin, Senator Kennedy made no bid for publicity, although the chief reporter for the *Irish Independent,* Michael Rooney, does recall having had a telephone call from Jacqueline Kennedy inviting him to visit the hotel to see her husband. Rooney, who is now editor of the paper, recalls with considerable regret his somewhat casual response to the invitation: "Three fellows are waiting for me now (it was Sunday) on the golf course and I am in serious trouble already for being late." He elicited a few facts about the Senatorial visit from Mrs. Kennedy, as a result of which a comparatively short paragraph appeared in the press.

What *was* John Kennedy doing in Ireland on that occasion? Was he fulfilling a desire to visit the country he loved so well, or was he showing the land of his forefathers to his wife? It may have been either, or both. He remained in Dublin the better part of a week, and despite his physical handicap, managed to get around quite a bit.

One of the unsung activities of Kennedy on that occasion was the address he gave at All Hallows College in Dublin on the effect of Communism on Catholic Poland. All Hallows, a training college for the clergy who are destined to serve abroad, sends many Irish priests to American dioceses. Apparently,

The Irish Heritage

The "Kennedy Homestead" built on the site from which President Kennedy's great-grandfather emigrated to the United States over a century and a half ago. John Brian O'Kennedy (standing at left) and teen-aged Nicholas Flavill (right) are related to the United States Kennedys.

U.P.I. Photograph

Lismore Castle looms high over neighboring Blackwater River—as dramatic and impressive today as it was when the last stone was put in place in King John's day in 1185. President Kennedy stayed at Lismore during his visit while a young Congressman.

Photo: Irish Tourist Bureau

The Book of Kells, 8th-Century illuminated manuscript, renders the Four Gospels in Latin. Its unknown scribes imparted to the work a transcendent beauty that has made the book world-renowned. Each day at Trinity College Library a new page is turned for visitors to see.

Photos: Bord Fáilte

John Kennedy's visit was the result of his wife's friendship with a Father Leonard from the college. The text of Kennedy's speech was not recorded; it was an *ex tempore* address which is still remembered by the senior officials of the college.

Liam Cosgrave, currently the opposition leader in the Irish Parliament, but at that time the Minister for External Affairs, gave a luncheon for Kennedy. Cosgrave still speaks with enthusiasm about the occasion, remembering his earnestness and eagerness and particularly his warmth and friendliness. John Kennedy referred repeatedly to Ireland, interpolating questions on Irish history into the discussion, though it was essentially of an international nature. Mrs. Costello, who acted as hostess for the Minister of External Affairs at the luncheon because Mrs. Cosgrave was ill, recalls that Kennedy bombarded her with questions about Irish history and Irish politics.

He was particularly interested in Roger Casement, the Irish patriot who had been hanged in England for treason following the Irish Rebellion of 1916. Casement had been in the British Colonial Service and was particularly active in the early days of the Congo. Prior to the 1916 Rising, he had been in touch with the Germans and was instrumental in arranging for German arms to be landed in Ireland to help the insurrection. At the time of the Kennedy visit, the Irish and British Governments were involved in discussions about the Casement memoirs, which were held by the British Government. Their return to Ireland had been demanded by the Irish, but the British were slow to return the writings of a man whom they had tried and convicted of treason.

Another subject Senator Kennedy discussed informally with Liam Cosgrave was the border question. For a long time one of the sorest points of Anglo-Irish relations, it has taken on qualities of the ridiculous alongside the world's concern about the possibility of nuclear war. Kennedy was keenly aware of the sentiment of the Irish both at home and abroad on this question. Although the Irish hopes to end partition reached their zenith when Kennedy was President, it never became a live issue even then. They still hope that with the United States leadership in international affairs the solution of the Irish border question will come as a result of American intervention.

Apart from Kennedy's official business in Ireland he also found time to play. An avid student of Shaw, O'Casey, and Joyce, he had learned that the Dublin pub was both the inspiration and the locale for much of the literary richness which had come out of Ireland. He spent a whole evening swapping stories in the pubs along the Dublin quays with Irish newspapermen. John Kennedy savored the Dublin of Joyce and O'Casey and thus more vividly than ever appreciated the richness of his Irish literary heritage.

In return, Kennedy left something with the Irish men and women whom he had met. While they all felt his humanity and friendliness, they recognized the steel in his makeup. It came as no great surprise to the people who met Kennedy in Ireland during his third visit that he was elected President of the United States. What did astound them was that as one of their own—and because of that—he could make it.

4

Presidential Visit

🍀 SHORTLY AFTER President De Valera invited President Kennedy to visit Ireland, and the date was set for June 26th, 1963, preparations were tackled with tremendous enthusiasm. The walls of thatch-roofed cottages were freshly whitewashed, choirs and bands in the towns and villages which he would visit practiced incessantly, women bought new outfits, and altogether throughout the country excitement reached fever pitch.

John F. Kennedy had caught the imagination of the Irish at home. They had considered his Presidential campaign, with its narrow victory, as a national triumph. His going to the land of his forefathers, therefore, was not merely to be a visit of the world's most powerful potentate, but rather the return of one of their own children who had reached the pinnacle of success in the mightiest nation in the world. He had, in effect, put Ireland back on the map by his victory and had proved the potential of an Irish heritage.

So intimate a part of Ireland had he become in the Irish mind that it is no wonder that the President of the Irish Republic addressed him in Gaelic on his arrival for the official visit. John Kennedy did not know Gaelic, but nonetheless, De Valera believed that he was formally taking him into the Irish family when he said:

"Mr. President, I welcome you in the name of all the people of Ireland. Your visit to Ireland gladdens the heart of every one of us and we are thankful to you.

"Mr. President," he went on in English, "I have thought it fitting that my first words of welcome to you should be in our native language; the language that was spoken throughout Ireland in the time of your ancestors; the language that was spoken by the great O'Kenedy clan of the Dal gCais, when, nine and a half centuries ago, almost on the spot on which we are now standing, under their mighty King Brian they smashed the invader and broke decisively the power of the Norseman; that language, Mr. President, which has never ceased to be spoken, will, please God, one day soon again become the everyday language of our people.

"Mr. President, our welcome to you is universal and heartfelt. We welcome you in the first place as the head, the chief executive and first citizen of the

President Kennedy's
Visit to Ireland
June 26-29, 1963

To the Irish, President Kennedy's visit seemed like a welcome return of one of their own children who had reached the pinnacle of success and, by so doing, had proved the potential of Irish heritage. Met at Dublin Airport by President De Valera, whose first welcome was spoken in Gaelic, Kennedy inspected a guard of honor.

Photo: Independent Newspapers, Ltd.

Kennedy drove with President De Valera to Arus an Uachtarain, residence of the President situated in famous Phoenix Park, Dublin.

Photo: Independent Newspapers, Ltd.

Replying to De Valera's welcome, Kennedy spoke feelingly of the Irish people who had emigrated but "kept a special place in their memories . . . of this green and misty island . . ." Photo: Independent Newspapers, Ltd.

President Kennedy with the President and Prime Minister of Ireland during the welcoming at the President's residence. Both De Valera and Lemass expressed then, and later, their strong feeling of personal friendship for the young man who had captured the imagination of every Irish citizen. Photo: Irish Times

Prime Minister Sean F. Lemass with Kennedy. In the fall of 1963, Lemass and his wife visited the United States at the invitation of President Kennedy. In an official statement after Kennedy's assassination, so soon to follow, the Prime Minister said, "the Irish people were united with nations 'round the world in a bitter sadness and sense of outrage . . ."

RIGHT TOP: *President Kennedy entertains President De Valera and Prime Minister Sean F. Lemass at the United States Embassy luncheon, June 28, 1963.*

RIGHT BOTTOM: *Next day, June 29, Kennedy received the freedom of the City of Dublin at the Mansion House.*
All photos: Independent Newspapers, Ltd.

Busy O'Connell Street in Dublin, named after Daniel O'Connell who was Dublin's Lord Mayor in 1829. Kennedy's love for the atmosphere of the place is reflected in his statement, "I can imagine nothing more pleasant than continuing day after day to drive through the streets of Dublin . . . I may come back and do it."

Photo: Irish Tourist Bureau

Dublin's ancient university, Trinity College, founded by Queen Elizabeth I of England.

Photo: Irish Tourist Bureau

great Republic of the West, on whose enlightened, wise and firm leadership now hangs the hope of the world.

"We welcome you in the second place, Mr. President, as the representative of that great country in which our people sought refuge when the misery of tyrant laws drove them from the motherland, and found a home in which they and their descendants prospered, won distinction and gave devoted service in return.

"Finally, we welcome you for yourself as the distinguished scion of our race who has won first place amongst his fellow countrymen, first in a nation of one hundred and eighty millions. We are proud of you, Mr. President; we admire the leadership you are giving; we hope that your return here to the ancient motherland will give you not merely pleasure, but renewed bodily strength and an ever more determined will in the pursuit of the safety and happiness of mankind. We pray God's inspiration and blessing upon you and upon your work.

"Long life to you and may God's blessing be on you, on your family and on your work."

John Kennedy replied:

"Mr. President, there are many reasons why I was anxious to accept your generous invitation, and to come to this country. As you said, eight of my great-grandparents left these shores in the space, almost, of months, and came to the United States. No country in the world, in the history of the world, has endured the hemorrhage which this island endured over a period of a few years for so many of her sons and daughters. These sons and daughters are scattered throughout the world, and they give this small island a family of millions upon millions who are scattered all over the globe, who have been among the best and most loyal citizens of the countries that they have gone to, but have also kept a special place in their memories, in many cases their ancestral memory, of this green and misty island, so, in a sense, all of them who visit Ireland come home."

The President then talked about Mr. De Valera, who had been born in America of a Spanish father and an Irish mother. De Valera's life was colorful, and courageous; he was one of the pioneers of the 1916 Rising, he had fought against the "Black and Tans" and had ended up in an English prison from which he had made a spectacular escape. He was the third president of the Irish Free State, created by the 1922 Treaty. In this capacity and on visits to the United States he had met Joseph Kennedy. So the American President continued:

"In addition, Mr. President, I am proud to visit here because of you, an old and valued friend of my father who has served with so much distinction, spreading over the period of a half-century; who has expressed in his own life and in the things that he stood for, the very best of Western thought, and equally important, Western action.

"And then I am glad to be here because this island still fulfills an historic assignment. There are Irishmen buried many thousands of miles from here who went on missions of peace, either as soldiers or as churchmen, who travelled throughout the world, carrying the gospel as so many Irish have done for so many hundreds of years.

"So, Mr. President, with the special pride that I feel in my own country, which has been so generous to so many immigrants from so many different countries, I want to say that I am happy to be here tonight."

On the day following his arrival, he set out for County Wexford. On the Crescent Quay in Wexford town he laid a wreath at the base of the Commodore John Barry Memorial, a tribute from a naval man to the "Father of the American Navy." The Barry Memorial is a nine-foot-high statue executed in bronze by the American sculptor Wheeler Williams. Mounted on a granite plinth decorated with plaques, it was presented by the people of the United States to the Irish nation and was unveiled by the President of Ireland on September 16th, 1956.

Kennedy was a great admirer of John Boyle O'Reilly, who had been a fellow Bostonian and one of the most colorful characters of his generation. O'Reilly was born in Drogheda, in Ireland, in 1844 and as a young man joined the Irish Republican Brotherhood, a secret organization closely allied to the Fenians. Later, he enlisted in a British cavalry regiment for the express purpose of sowing seeds of discord among the troops. His efforts were eminently successful; he had a number of regiments on the very threshold of mutiny when he was discovered by the authorities. O'Reilly was arrested in Dublin, where he was tried and sentenced to be shot; his sentence was later commuted to 20 years in a penal settlement in Australia. O'Reilly managed to escape from the settlement in a whaler and made his way to the United States. In Boston he became the editor of a Catholic newspaper, *The Pilot.*

O'Reilly's love of Ireland never waned, and from his new position he planned the escape of Irish political prisoners from the Australian penal colonies. He was one of the prime movers in the "Catalpa" expedition, one of the most daring in history.

The following excerpt is taken from a book called *The Expedition of the Catalpa:* "One hundred years after the Declaration of Independence an American whaling Captain, George S. Anthony, commemorated the event by enforcing another Declaration of Independence which set free the Irish political prisoners who were sentenced to a lifetime of servitude in the English penal colony in Australia.

"In April, 1875, the *Catalpa* left New Bedford in one of the most boldly conceived and audacious expeditions against the English Government ever planned. This was the only important Fenian conspiracy which was entirely successful. The plan to

President Kennedy in Wexford

In anticipation of the President's visit the walls of many a thatch-roofed cottage like this one were given a fresh coat of whitewash. Photo: Irish Tourist Bureau

Kennedy's visit to Wexford and nearby Dunganstown was
a sentimental journey back to the section from which his
great-great-grandfather Patrick Kennedy left for the
United States. Surrounded by the Chairman and Town
Commissioners of New Ross and the Mayors of Waterford,
Clonmel, and Kilkenny, Kennedy gave to the people of
the town a speech filled with his own special brand of
warmth and humor.

AT RIGHT: On nearby Wexford Crescent Quay, Kennedy
lays a wreath at base of memorial to John Barry, Irish-
American seaman who distinguished himself in combat at
sea during the American Revolution. With President
Kennedy are Thomas Byrne, Mayor of Wexford; Mr.
Frank Aiken, Minister for External Affairs; Mr. Matthew
McCloskey, U.S. Ambassador to Ireland.

Photos: Independent Newspapers, Ltd.

President Kennedy's drive from Wexford Town to the little town of Dunganstown, for an informal family reunion, was a triumphal journey along flag-decked streets. The crowd roared its greetings. With him rides Mr. Frank Aiken, Irish Minister for External Affairs.

Photo: Irish Times

At the farm home of Mrs. Mary Kennedy Ryan, in the
midst of cousins from far and near who had come to honor
their illustrious young relative, Kennedy proposed a toast:
"We will drink a cup of tea to all the Kennedys who have
gone away and to all who have remained at home."

Photo: Independent Newspapers, Ltd.

The President surrounded by Wexford County relatives.
From left to right: Mrs. Mary Ryan, President Kennedy,
Miss Mary Ryan, Mrs. Margaret Whitty, Miss Joan Kir-
wan, Miss Margaret Kirwan. The family resemblance is
notable. Photo: Independent Newspapers, Ltd.

rescue the prisoners was suggested to John Devoy by John Boyle O'Reilly, who had previously escaped from the same Australian penal colony on a whaling ship.

"John Devoy rallied the rank and file of the Clann na Gael and they purchased the *Catalpa* on March 13, 1875, for $5,500. The estimated cost, though, of the voyage was $25,858.

"John Devoy, who had taken an active part in planning the expedition, was present to wish the crew God-speed. On April 17, 1876, the successful escape of six prisoners was accomplished and four months later on August 19, 1876 the *Catalpa* anchored off Castle Garden, New York."

After placing a wreath on John Barry's memorial, Kennedy concluded:

"And I am proud to come here ... because it makes me even prouder of my own country. My country welcomed so many sons and daughters of so many countries, Irish and Scandinavian, Germans, Italian and all the rest, and gave them a fair chance and a fair opportunity. The Speaker of the House of Representatives is of Irish descent. The leader of the Senate is also of Irish descent. And what is true of the Irish has been true of dozens of other people. In Ireland I think you see something of what is so great about the United States, and I must say that in the United States, through millions of your sons and daughters and cousins, twenty-five million, in fact, you see something of what is great about Ireland."

While in Wexford, the President visited the quay in New Ross from which his great-grandfather Patrick Kennedy had set sail for America 115 years before. A formal reception had been arranged by the town mayor, Mr. Andrew Minahan, but John Kennedy's spirit was so infectious that the proceedings became most informal.

One of the highlights of the Wexford trip was Kennedy's return visit to Dunganstown, the family homestead where his cousins live. With enthusiasm and friendliness the President remembered his previous visit with his relatives and had with him a photograph he had taken many years before. He intended to match up his cousins with those in the picture.

Before his arrival, his cousin's home had been specially prepared. The yard of Mrs. Ryan's house had been concreted and a bountiful spread prepared with the cooperation of the neighbors. Salmon sandwiches were on the menu. As the President was eating one, he casually remarked to his second cousin, Jimmy Kennedy, "Did you 'poach' that salmon this morning?"

Although the President was the first of the more prosperous Kennedys to visit the house, Jimmy reminded him that his paternal grandfather had returned on a visit in 1906. Jimmy also told the President, "Sure you were only a tall slight lad when you were here before."

The President proposed a toast: "We will drink a

cup of tea to all the Kennedys who have gone away and to all who have remained at home." His obvious enjoyment was infectious, and what had been planned as an official occasion became a happy family reunion; security measures and the demands of the official program went by the board.

As he left, he talked with the local schoolchildren lined up in a body outside the farm, but not before he had invited all to join the informal festivities.

County Wexford will always remember the Kennedy visit. The official guide to the county now contains the following passage: "No one will fail to grasp the significance of the visit of the late President of the mighty United States of America to this ancient town in the last days of June, 1963. We who are now living have had the privilege of seeing, I submit, Wexford's greatest day. He was welcomed as an honored and invited guest to our town. He was welcomed as the Chief Executive of the Bulwark of Freedom, the Land of the Free and the Home of the Brave. He was welcomed as the great-grandson of a County Wexfordman who emigrated to America, and he was welcomed for his own integrity and worth. The Freedom of this ancient Borough of Wexford was conferred on John F. Kennedy, and when one considers the vicissitudes through which Wexford has passed in its time, isn't it a splendid thing to reflect that John F. Kennedy was one of our own?"

From Wexford, Kennedy went to Cork city, the

Cork City, County of Cork

The ancient city of Cork, capital of Southern Ireland, on the beautiful River Lee, where for John F. Kennedy the famous Bells of Shandon rang out—a sound that stirs the heart of many a returning exile.

Photo: Irish Tourist Bureau

ON THE FOLLOWING PAGE: *Cork's welcome to Kennedy was a joyous one; his car was showered with rose petals and confetti, and at every corner pipe bands and fiddlers, melodeon players, and brass bands gave out a tuneful greeting.* Photo: Liam Kennedy and Sons

*Cobh, seaport town of County Cork, lies fourteen miles to
the south of Cork City, and has a harbor where many
ocean liners drop anchor. Here: an ancient clock tower,
topped by weather vane.*   Photo: Irish Tourist Bureau

Youghal, County Cork, finest seaside resort for the section, and a haven for fishermen who catch, in the Blackwater River, some of the finest salmon in the world.

Photo: Irish Tourist Bureau

capital of Southern Ireland. This was not his first visit to that city by the Lee; when he was at Lismore Castle years before, he had watched the beautiful river flow by and was familiar with both its poetic and its historic significance. On this visit the famous Bells of Shandon pealed out for him, and that sound in itself stirs the heart of many a returning exile.

In Cork, the Guard of Honor consisted of Irish soldiers who had fought in the Congo. His welcome to the city was a joyous one; his car was showered with rose petals and confetti, and at every corner pipe bands and fiddlers, melodeon players and brass bands all gave him a wild reception. The Freedom of the City was conferred on him, and as he did everywhere, he conducted all the proceedings in an informal way.

On his way to the City Hall, he met four of his Fitzgerald cousins. Commenting on this fact, he said: "Coming here today I met four rather angry Fitzgeralds, and they said they were tired of hearing about the Kennedys of New Ross, and asked what about the Fitzgeralds. I said that that was because my grandfather, John Fitzgerald, who was Mayor of Boston, used to tell everybody he was from Limerick and Donegal and Galway or wherever . . ."

In the formal part of his reply to the Cork officials the President said:

"Most countries send out oil, iron, steel or gold, some others, crops, but Ireland has only one export, and that is people. They have gone all over the

United States, and the United States has been generous to them, and I think it is not unfair to say that
they have been generous themselves with their sons
and daughters to the United States."

On his return to Dublin, Kennedy laid a wreath
at Arbour Hill. In a small green plot on this hallowed
ground lie the remains of the executed leaders of
the small band of men who went out to fight the
might of an empire in 1916. These were the men
who laid the foundation of Irish freedom. On leaving
Ireland, Kennedy referred to the Arbour Hill ceremony and said: "The highlight? That was the memorial service at Arbour Hill." The President was particularly impressed by the ceremonial drill of the
Guard of Honor for this occasion and asked that a
film be made of it. He had in mind introducing a
similar memorial drill at Arlington Cemetery. The
first use of this drill was when Mrs. Kennedy sent for
the Irish Army Cadets who had performed the ceremony before the President to come to Arlington,
where they went through the same drill sequence—
this time *for* the President.

After visiting Arbour Hill, President Kennedy addressed the Houses of Parliament. He was the first
President of the United States to do so, and the
second non-Irish speaker ever to address that body,
the first being Pandit Nehru a few years previously.

In welcoming the President, the Ceann Comhairle
(Speaker) said that "in ordinary circumstances it

would be an occasion of pride and privilege for an Irishman to welcome the President of the United States of America to an Irish Parliament. But, Mr. President, this is not an ordinary occasion. Your great personality elevates it far above that level. It is an occasion unique as an event in Irish history—it is an international gesture of kindness and goodwill of inestimable value. When the citizen who presides over the great American people of the United States shares with the people of Ireland the heritage of blood, of name and tradition, then the event is enhanced almost beyond measure."

The President mentioned in his speech to the Irish Parliament the Battle of Fredericksburg, the Fighting Irish (the 69th New York Regiment) and Brigadier General Thomas Francis Meagher, who led the Irish in the battle during the American Civil War.

"Mr. Speaker, Prime Minister, Members of Parliament: I am grateful for your welcome and for that of your countrymen.

"The 13th day of December, 1862, will be a day long remembered in American history. At Fredericksburg, Virginia, thousands of men fought and died on one of the bloodiest battlefields of the American Civil War. One of the most brilliant stories of that day was written by a band of 1,200 men who went into battle wearing a green sprig in their hats. They bore a proud heritage and a special courage, given to those who had long fought for the cause of freedom. I am referring, of course, to the Irish Brigade. As General Robert E. Lee, the great military leader of the Southern Confederate forces, was reported to have said of this group of men after the battle: 'The gallant stand which this bold brigade made on the heights of Fredericksburg is well-known. Never were men so brave. They ennobled their race by their splendid gallantry on that desperate occasion. Their brilliant, though hopeless assaults on our lines excited the hearty applause of our officers and soldiers.'

"Of the 1,200 men who took part in that assault, 280 survived the battle. The Irish Brigade was led into battle on that occasion by Brigadier General Thomas F. Meagher, who had participated in the unsuccessful Irish uprising of 1848, was captured by the British and sent in a prison ship to Australia, from whence he finally came to America. In the fall of 1862, after serving with distinction and gallantry in some of the toughest fighting of this most bloody struggle, the Irish Brigade was presented with a new set of flags. In the city-ceremony, the city chamberlain gave them the motto 'The Union, our Country, and Ireland Forever.' Their old ones having been torn to shreds by bullets in previous battles, Captain Richard McGee took possession of these flags on September 2nd in New York City and arrived with them at the Battle of Fredericksburg and carried them in the battle. Today, in recognition of what these gallant Irishmen and what millions of other Irish have done for my country, and through the generosity of the Fighting 69th, I would like to present one of these flags to the people of Ireland."

The President then unveiled the flag.

"As you can see, gentlemen, the battle honors of the Brigade include Fredericksburg, Chancellorsville, Yorktown, Fair Oaks, Gaines Hill, Allen's Farm, Savage's Station, White Oak Bridge, Glendale, Malvern Hills, Antietam, Gettysburg, Bristoe's Station.

"This elegant building, as you know, was once the property of the Fitzgerald family, but I have not come here to claim it. Of all the new relations I have discovered on this trip, I regret to say that no one has yet found any link between me and a great Irish patriot, Lord Edward Fitzgerald. Lord Edward, however, did not like to stay here in his family home because, as he wrote his mother: 'Leinster House does not inspire the brightest ideas.' That was a long time ago, however. It has also been said by some that a few of the features of this stately mansion served to inspire similar features in the White House in Washington. Whether this is true or not, I know that the White House was designed by James Hoban, a noted Irish-American architect, and I have no doubt that he would make it more homelike for any President of Irish descent. It was a long wait, but I appreciate the effort.

"There is also an unconfirmed rumor that Hoban,

was never fully paid for his work on the White House. If this proves to be true, I will speak to our Secretary of the Treasury about it, although I hear this body is not particularly interested in the subject of revenues.

"I am proud to be the first American President to visit Ireland during his term of office, proud to be addressing this distinguished assembly, and proud of the welcome that you have given. My presence and your welcome, however, only symbolize the many and enduring links which have bound the Irish and the Americans since the earliest days.

"Benjamin Franklin, the envoy of the American Revolution, who was also born in Boston, was received by the Irish Parliament in 1772. It was neither independent nor free from discrimination at the time, but Franklin reported its members 'disposed to be friends of America.' 'By joining our interests with theirs,' he said, 'a more equitable treatment . . . might be obtained for both nations.'

"Our interests have been joined ever since. Franklin sent leaflets to Irish Freedom Fighters. O'Connell was influenced by Washington, and Emmet influenced Lincoln. Irish volunteers played so predominant a role in the American army that Lord Mountjoy lamented in the British Parliament: 'We have lost America through the Irish.' John Barry, whose statue was honored yesterday, and whose sword is in my office, was only one who fought for liberty in

America to set an example for liberty in Ireland. . . .
Yesterday was the 117th anniversary of the birth of
Charles Stewart Parnell—whose grandfather fought
under Barry and whose mother was born in America."

Parnell and John Dillon went on their memorable
mission of charity to the United States in December
1876, where a large sum was raised for the suffering
people. The *New York Herald* on this occasion did
noble work by opening a relief fund in its columns,
which it headed with the magnificent sum of twenty
thousand dollars. The *Irish World,* also, for its un-
ceasing efforts on behalf of the famine-stricken people, and the immense sums of money it was instrumental in raising at that period, and every week
during the existence of the Land League, has merited
the undying gratitude of the Irish people. The
United States Government gave a warship—the *Constitution*—to bring over the supplies of provisions
collected in the States for the same charitable object.

"Parnell, at the age of 34," the President continued,
"was invited to address the American Congress on
the cause of Irish freedom. 'I have seen since I have
been in this country,' he said, 'so many tokens of the
good wishes of the American people toward Ireland . . .' And today, 83 years later, I can say to you
that I have seen in this country so many tokens of
good wishes of the Irish people toward America.

"And so it is that our two nations, divided by
distance, have been united by history. No people

ever believed more deeply in the cause of Irish freedom than the people of the United States. And no country contributed more to building my own than your sons and daughters. They came to our shores in a mixture of hope and agony, and I would not underrate the difficulties of their course once they arrived in the United States. They left behind hearts, fields, and a nation yearning to be free. It is no wonder that James Joyce described the Atlantic as a bowl of bitter tears, and an earlier poet wrote: 'They are going, going, going, and we cannot bid them stay.'

"But today this is no longer the country of hunger and famine that those immigrants left behind. It is not rich and its progress is not yet complete, but it is, according to statistics, one of the best-fed countries in the world. Nor is it any longer a country of persecution, political or religious. It is a free country, and that is why any American feels at home.

"There are those who regard this history of past strife and exile as better forgotten, but to use the phrase of Yeats: 'Let us not casually reduce that great past to a trouble of fools, for we need not feel the bitterness of the past to discover its meaning for the present and the future.'

"And it is the present and the future of Ireland that today hold so much promise to my nation as well as to yours, and, indeed, to all mankind, for the Ireland of 1963, one of the youngest of nations, and the oldest of civilizations, has discovered that the achievement of nationhood is not an end, but a beginning. In the years since independence you have undergone a new and peaceful revolution, an economic and industrial revolution, transforming the face of this land, while still holding to the old spiritual and cultural values. You have modernized your economy, harnessed your rivers, diversified your industry, liberalized your trade, electrified your farms, accelerated your rate of growth, and improved the living standards of your people.

"Other nations of the world in whom Ireland has long invested her people and her children are now investing their capital as well as their vacations here in Ireland. This revolution is not yet over, nor will it be, I am sure, until a fully modern Irish economy fully shares in world prosperity."

The President then turned his attention to another of Ireland's statesmen, Henry Grattan, who won for the Irish nation at least a British promise of freedom, although it was quickly broken.

"One hundred and eighty-three years ago, Henry Grattan, demanding the more independent Irish Parliament that would always bear his name, denounced those who were satisfied merely by new grants of economic opportunity. 'A country,' he said, 'enlightened as Ireland, chartered as Ireland, armed as Ireland, and injured as Ireland, will be satisfied with nothing less than liberty.' And today, I am cer-

Back to Dublin

Returning to Dublin from County Cork by helicopter, the President landed in Phoenix Park, where 1,760 acres of gardens, walks, playing fields, and even a racecourse offer pleasure to Dubliners.

Photo: Independent Newspapers, Ltd.

The President acknowledges the cheers from the crowd at Arbour Hill, Dublin, where he came to lay a wreath on the graves of the leaders of the Easter Week Rebellion of 1916. With the President, at left, Prime Minister Sean F. Lemass and, at right, Lt. General Sean McEoin, Chief of Staff and formerly U.N. Commander in Chief in the Congo. Photo: Independent Newspapers, Ltd.

After the ceremony, which included an impressive cere-
monial drill by Irish Army Cadets, Kennedy takes the
salute with other members of the military group.

Photo: Independent Newspapers, Ltd.

National University, Dublin, from which institution the President received an honorary Doctor of Laws degree.
Photo: Irish Tourist Bureau

Interior of the Library of Trinity College, which houses a notable collection of manuscripts concerning the history of Ireland. Trinity also bestowed an honorary degree upon the President during his visit. Photo: Irish Tourist Bureau

tain, free Ireland, a full-fledged member of the world community, where some are not yet freed, and where some counsel an acceptance of tyranny—free Ireland will not be satisfied with anything less than liberty.

"I am glad, therefore, that Ireland is moving in the mainstream of current world events. For I sincerely believe that your future is as promising as your past is proud, and that your destiny lies not as a peaceful island in a sea of troubles, but as a maker and shaper of world peace.

"For self-determination can no longer mean isolation; and the achievement of national independence today means withdrawal from the old status only to return to the world scene with a new one. New nations can build with their former governing powers the same kind of fruitful relationship that Ireland has established with Great Britain—a relationship founded on equality and mutual interests. And no nation, large or small, can be indifferent to the fate of others, near or far. Modern economics, weaponry and communications have made us realize more than ever that we are one human family and this one planet is our home.

'The world is large,' wrote John Boyle O'Reilly,

> 'The world is large when its weary leagues
>   two loving hearts divide,
> but the world is small when your enemy
>   is loose on the other side.'

"The world is even smaller today, though the enemy of John Boyle O'Reilly is no longer a hostile power. Indeed, across the gulfs and barriers that now divide us, we must remember that there are no permanent enemies. Hostility today is a fact, but it is not a ruling law. The supreme reality of our times is our indivisibility as children of God and our common vulnerability on this planet.

"Some may say that all this means little to Ireland. In an age when 'history moves with the tramp of earthquake feet,' in an age when a handful of men and nations have the power to devastate mankind, in an age when the needs of the developing nations are so large and staggering that even the richest lands often groan with the burden of assistance—in such an age, it may be asked, how can a nation as small as Ireland play much of a role on the world stage?

"I would remind those who ask that question, including those in other small countries, of these words of one of the great orators of the English language:

" 'All the world owes much to the little "five feet high" nations. The greatest art of the world was the work of little nations. The most enduring literature of the world came from little nations. The heroic deeds that thrill humanity through generations were the deeds of little nations fighting for their freedom. And, oh, yes, the salvation of mankind came through a little nation.'

"Ireland has already set an example and a standard

for other small nations to follow. This has never been a rich or powerful country, and yet since earliest times, its influence on the world has been rich and powerful. No larger nation did more to keep Christianity and Western culture alive in their darkest centuries. No larger nation did more to spark the cause of independence in America. Indeed, around the world. And no larger nation has ever provided the world with more literary and artistic genius.

"This is an extraordinary country. George Bernard Shaw, speaking as an Irishman, summed up an approach to life:

" 'Other peoples,' he said, 'see things and say: "Why?". . . . But I dream things that never were—and I say: "Why not?" '

"It is that quality of the Irish, the remarkable combination of hope, confidence and imagination that is needed more than ever today. The problems of the world cannot possibly be solved by skeptics or cynics whose horizons are limited by the obvious realities. We need men who can dream of things that never were, and ask why not. It matters not how small a nation is that seeks world peace and freedom, for, to paraphrase a citizen of my country: 'The humblest nation of all the world, when clad in the armor of a righteous cause, is stronger than all the host of Error.'

"Ireland is clad in the cause of national and human liberty with peace. To the extent that the peace is disturbed by conflict between the former colonial powers and the new and developing nations, Ireland's role is unique. For every new nation knows that Ireland was the first of the small nations in the 20th century to win its struggle for independence, and that the Irish have traditionally sent their doctors and technicians and soldiers and priests to help other lands to keep their liberty alive. At the same time, Ireland is part of Europe, associated with the Council of Europe, progressing in the context of Europe, and a prospective member of an expanded European Common Market. Thus Ireland has excellent relations with both the new and the old, the confidence of both sides and an opportunity to act where the actions of greater powers might be looked upon with suspicion.

"The central issue of freedom, however, is between those who believe in self-determination and those in the East who would impose on others the harsh and oppressive Communist system; and here your nation wisely rejects the role of a go-between or a mediator. Ireland pursues an independent course in foreign policy, but it is not neutral between liberty and tyranny and never will be.

"For knowing the meaning of foreign domination, Ireland is the example and inspiration to those enduring endless years of oppression. It was fitting and appropriate that this nation played a leading role in censuring the suppression of the Hungarian Revolution, for how many times was Ireland's quest for freedom suppressed only to have that quest renewed by the succeeding generation? Those who suffer beyond that wall I saw on Wednesday in Berlin must not despair of their future. Let them remember the constancy, the faith, the endurance and the final success of the Irish. And let them remember, as I heard sung by your sons and daughters yesterday in Wexford, the words 'The Boys of Wexford, who fought with heart and hand, to burst in twain the galling chain and free our native land.'

"The major forum for your nation's greatest role in world affairs is that of the protector of the weak and voice of the small, the United Nations. From Cork to the Congo, from Galway to the Gaza Strip, from this legislative assembly to the United Nations, Ireland is sending its most talented men to do the world's most important work—the work of peace.

"In a sense, this export of talent is in keeping with an historic Irish role. But you no longer go as exiles and emigrants, but for the service of your country and, indeed, of all men. Like the Irish missionaries of medieval days, like the wild geese after the Battle of the Boyne, you are not content to sit by your fireside while others are in need of your help. Nor are you content with the recollections of the past when you face the responsibilities of the present.

"Twenty-six sons of Ireland have died in the Congo; many others have been wounded. I pay tribute to them and to all of you for your commitment and dedication to world order. And their sacrifice reminds us all that we must not falter now. . . .

"Ireland's influence in the United Nations is far greater than your relative size. You have not hesitated to take the lead on such sensitive issues as the Kashmir dispute, and you sponsored that most vital resolution, adopted by the General Assembly, which opposed the spread of nuclear arms to any nation not now possessing them, urging an international agreement with inspection and control, and I pledge to you that the United States of America will do all in its power to achieve such an agreement and fulfill your resolution.

"I speak of these matters today not because Ireland is unaware of its role, but I think it important that you know that we know what you have done, and I speak to remind the other small nations that they, too, can and must help build a world peace. They, too, as we all are, are dependent on the United Nations for security, for an equal chance to be heard, for progress toward a world made safe for diversity. The peace-keeping machinery of the United Nations cannot work without the help of the smaller nations, nations whose forces threaten no one, and whose forces can thus help create a world in which no nation is threatened.

"Great powers have their responsibilities and their burdens, but the smaller nations of the world must fulfill their obligations as well. A great Irish poet once wrote: 'I believe profoundly in the future of Ireland, that this is an isle of destiny, that that destiny will be glorious, and that when our hour has come we will have something to give the world.'

"My friends, Ireland's hour has come. You have something to give to the world, and that is a future of peace and freedom."

The President had two further honors bestowed on him in St. Patrick's Hall in Dublin Castle. The Castle was built in the 13th century and was the bastion of English rule in Ireland. It was the official residence of the King of England's viceroy and the center of Government administration. St. Patrick's Hall was built in the 18th century on the site of King Henry III's Great Hall. Since the foundation of the Irish Free State, it has formed the principal room in the magnificent group of State Apartments used for great occasions of state. In 1938 Joseph P. Kennedy received his honorary degree from the National University in the same building.

John F. Kennedy received honorary Doctorate degrees from both the National University and the famed Trinity College, more accurately described as Dublin University.

Receiving degrees from the rival universities in the same hall gave the President an opportunity to show both his amazing adaptability and his wonderful sense of humor. When receiving the Doctor of Laws degree from National he donned a gown of scarlet and purple with a hood of green and purple and a doctor's black flat cap on his head. For Trinity he promptly changed to robes of scarlet with a gown and hood of pink. Addressing both faculties after the ceremony, he spoke candidly: "I want to say how pleased I am to have this association with these two great Universities. I now feel equally part of both, and if they ever have a game of Gaelic football or hurling, *I shall cheer for Trinity and pray for National*." Only someone very familiar with the rivalry between the two universities could have made such a remark. Trinity has always been the stronghold of the small Protestant population in Ireland, and when the National University was founded, its purpose was to be a Catholic bulwark concerned with the Gaelic tradition.

The President went on:

"It is appropriate to have this opportunity to form this association, because Ireland and education have been synonymous for nearly 2,000 years. For so many hundreds of years, this country had colleges and universities of 2,000, 3,000, and 4,000 students in the darkest ages of Europe, which served as the core, as the foundation, for what became the enlightenment and the religious revival of Europe. This country was wise enough to see in days that were past, that when it finally became independent it would need educated men and women. Democracy is a difficult kind of government. It requires the highest qualities of self-discipline, restraint, a willingness to make commitments and sacrifices for the general interest, and also it requires knowledge. My own country, in its earliest days, put the greatest emphasis on the development of education for its citizens. In the Northwest Ordinance, which was drafted by Thomas Jefferson and John Adams, it was provided that a section of land would be set aside in every 30 sections in order to educate the people. Thomas Jefferson once said: 'If you expect the people to be ignorant and free, you expect what never was and never will be.' And in the heights of the Civil War, when the outcome was most uncertain, and the results in doubt, the United States Congress, under the leadership of Abraham Lincoln, passed the Morrill Act, which established our land-grant colleges, and which set aside public land in every state in order to maintain a state college and state university. We have just recently celebrated the 100th anniversary and we now have, in every one of our states, universities which have educated our sons and daughters and helped make it possible to maintain self-government. So education, these two great schools, the City of Dublin, the country of Ireland, the future of the West, all are closely intertwined, and I can assure you that there are no greater honors that you could give me as the President of the United States than to have received the two distinctions which I hold today and shall always value."

On his last day in Ireland, President Kennedy went to the ancient city of Galway. There he visited the Collegiate Church of St. Nicholas where, according

Galway

The swans of Galway, a familiar sight in Western Ireland's main city, which is the gateway to the moor and mountain country of Connemora. Photo: Irish Tourist Bureau

Arriving at Eyre Square,
Galway

*On his last day in Ireland, Kennedy visited the ancient
city of Galway, where he passed through a crowd of 80,000
while the bells of the Collegiate Church of St. Nicholas
pealed "The Star-Spangled Banner." It was in this church,
it is told, that Christopher Columbus attended Mass
before setting out on his voyage of discovery to America.*
Photo: Independent Newspapers, Ltd.

Visitors to Galway visit the ancient Spanish Arch. The Spanish influence evident in much of Galway's architecture stems from the period when Galway was a northerly port for heavy sea trade between France and Spain and Ireland. Photo: Bord Fáilte

to tradition, Columbus heard Mass before setting out on his voyage of discovery to America. As Kennedy drew near the Church, he passed through a crowd of 80,000 while the bells pealed "The Star-Spangled Banner."

Galway City was long thought to be the place where the phrase "Lynch Law" originated. The Lynches were one of the so-called 13 tribes of Galway and over a period of 169 years had something like 84 mayors of the city. Even prior to the Spanish Armada in 1588, very close ties existed between Galway and Spain. It was from Lynch castle that one of the Lynches, a mayor of Galway, hanged his own son, thereby, according to the old story, giving rise to "Lynch Law." It happened that in 1493 Mayor Lynch was on a visit to the English court and his son was deputizing for him in his absence. There came to Galway at the time a young Spanish nobleman who was unwise enough to fall in love with young Lynch's fiancée. Lynch, in a rage, murdered the Spaniard, but so great was his popularity in the town that the authorities chose to disregard the crime.

On his return from England, the Mayor was utterly shocked at what had transpired and had his own son tried for murder. However, the town officials were so fond of the boy that when he was found guilty they attempted to reverse his sentence and let him go free. Afraid that they would free the boy by force, the Mayor seized his own son and hanged him from one of the windows of the castle while a raging mob in the street below protested loudly.

It was in this historic city that President Kennedy said: "If the day was clear enough and if you went down to the Bay and you looked west and your sight was good enough you would see Boston, Massachusetts . . .

"I don't know what it is about you that causes me to think that nearly everybody in Boston comes from Galway. They are not shy about it at all. I want to express, as we are about to leave here, how much this visit has meant.

"It is strange that so many years could pass and so many generations pass and still some of us who came on this trip could come home here to Ireland and feel ourselves at home and not feel ourselves in a strange country, but feel ourselves among neighbors even though we are separated by generations, by time and by thousands of miles.

"So you have made all of us feel. You send us home covered with gifts which we can barely carry, but most of all you send us home with the warmest memories of you and your country."

As President Kennedy's motorcade drove back through the cheering crowds to his waiting helicopter at Salthill, a band played "Galway Bay." Out on the Bay itself the Irish naval corvette *Cliona* was riding at anchor, dressed in his honor, with a crescent of Aran and Claddagh fishing vessels around her.

From Galway the President went to Limerick, where he was welcomed by the woman mayor, Mrs. Frances Condell, who received the Presidential party on a platform at Greenpark Racecourse: "Mr. President, I wonder if it is possible for you to realize the great privilege and honor it is for me, on behalf of my fellow Councillors, citizens and all those present here this afternoon, to welcome you to our City and County of Limerick.

"Your unexpected but sincerely hoped-for decision to come to Limerick was acclaimed with the widest jubilation and we thank you warmly, Sir, for changing your plans at the last moment to permit us this privilege and the joy of meeting you and the other members of your family on our own soil . . .

"While listening in awed admiration to your speeches in Germany on Wednesday last and later upon your arrival in Dublin, my mind was directed towards your words and the reasons for your work and visit to Europe.

"We in Ireland owe much to the reasoning of another man, who returned to Ireland to give us a Faith and a Freedom of mind, for which you and I, Sir, are proud to continue fighting and to practice in our lives.

"I refer, of course, to our Irish Saint Patrick and to the legend of the shamrock with its three leaves, growing from one stem.

"As I listened to you, Mr. President, I could not

but interpret your reasoning by a modern idea based on the symbol of the shamrock and our Christian belief; that you and your people with us see three good reasons for living, for determined unity and for working together towards world peace,- three good reasons springing from our common hereditary stem, which inspires us toward your aims and the aims of all free people, which we hope you will achieve, Sir, as St. Patrick did in the name of God."

Mrs. Condell justly referred to her city as historical. However, as she continued her address she touched on more intimate and recent events.

"It was from our docks, Sir, that many emigrant ships set sail for your shores and from which point of departure our people became yours.

"That time of great exodus is over, thank God, and I'm sure you'll agree with me that you have enough of us over there to keep you happy and to assure you of our faithful support at all times.

"The day has come when the point of departure and arrival has transferred itself for us, some 15 miles westward, and in keeping with modern times, to an airport. Limerick has benefited immeasurably by its close proximity to Shannon Airport which, for the last 18 years, has served as a major international airport, and as a strong connecting link between our old world and your new one.

"Because of our proximity to the airport, also, we have the pleasure of welcoming each year many of

Limerick

The children of Limerick greet President Kennedy with obvious enthusiasm.

Photo: Independent Newspapers, Ltd.

Limerick, fifteen miles from Shannon Airport, was the President's last stop before departure. One of the city's most impressive structures is King John's Castle, shown here, which was built in 1210. It stands on the banks of the beautiful River Shannon. Photo: Irish Tourist Bureau

*The lady mayor of Limerick, Mrs. Frances Condell, was
the only official on the distaff side to officiate at a formal
welcoming ceremony. She said, in part, "... our enthusiasm to have you come to Limerick was set alight and
fanned by a true Irish wind of affection and admiration ..."* Photo: Irish Times

your fellow countrymen and our returning emigrants. Now with the setting up of the Industrial Estate at Shannon in which five American firms have established themselves, we have seen the introduction of a new type of American who is taking his place in our civic and social life, and who is bringing to our people the skills and techniques of industry.

"You see, Mr. President, we, the women of Limerick City and County, feel that we have a special claim on you! We claim the Fitzgerald in you, and are extremely proud of your heritage. Over there, you see a large number of your relatives and connections who have come to greet you—on the distaff side ... These good people have come to show our Limerick claim on you, and by their presence they prove that the Fitzgeralds are proud of their own Rose and her dynamic father, 'Honey Fitz,' your reputable and colorful and most successful grandfather.

"You and your wife and family have become a symbol to us here in this country and an example of family life based on Irish heritage ..."

In reply Kennedy said: "... You can be proud of them (Americans of Irish descent) and they are proud of you. Even though a good many years have passed since most of them left, they still retain the strongest sentiments of affection for this country and I hope that this visit that we have been able to make has reminded them not only of their past, but also that there in Ireland the word 'freedom,' the word 'independence,' the whole sentiment of a nation, are perhaps stronger than in almost any place in the world.

"I don't think that I have passed through a more impressive ceremony than the one I experienced yesterday in Dublin when I went with your Prime Minister to put a wreath on the graves of the men who died in 1916, . . . to see your President, who has played such a distinguished part, whose life is so tied up with the life of this island in this century—all this has made the past very real and has made the present very hopeful. So I carry with me as I go the warmest sentiments of appreciation toward all of you. This is a great country, with a great people, and I know that when I am back in Washington I can—well, I will not see you, but I will see you in my mind and feel all of your good wishes, as we all will in our hearts. . . ."

From Limerick City the President made the short journey to Shannon to bid farewell to the Irish.

At Shannon Airport, where the Clare County Council presented to him a piece of old Irish silver, President Kennedy took leave with these words:

". . . Ireland is an unusual place. What happened 500 or 1,000 years ago is yesterday; although we are on the other side of the Atlantic, 3,000 miles away, we are next door. While there may be those removed by two or three generations from Ireland, they may have left 100 years ago their people, and yet when I ask how many people have relatives in America, nearly everyone holds up their hands. So Ireland is a very special place.

"It has fulfilled in the past a very special role. It is in a very real sense the mother of a great many people, a great many millions of people, and in a sense a great many nations, and what gives me the greatest satisfaction and pride, being of Irish descent, is the realization that even today this very small island sends thousands, literally thousands, of its sons and daughters to the ends of the globe to carry on an historic task which Ireland asumed 1,400 or 1,500 years ago.

"Well, I am going to come back and see old Shannon's face again, and I am taking, as I go to America, all of you with me. Thank you."

Epilogue

🍀 IN DUNGANSTOWN the evening of November 22, 1963, Josie Ryan was sitting by the fire on the same stool where the President had sat a short time previously. She heard the announcement on the radio. A few minutes later the nearby members of her family began collecting. The curate came from the local church where so many of the Kennedy ancestors had been baptized, and although there was no keening, nothing suggestive of the old-fashioned Irish wake about the gathering, the feeling of intimate family loss was profound. Around the kitchen and the living room were many remembrances of the President. There were photographs of the visit, a picture of Jacqueline Kennedy, a letter of thanks in a beautiful frame from the White House.

Over the television came the words of President De Valera: "You will all have heard of the tragic death of President Kennedy. I am here simply to give public expression to our common sorrow. We sympathize with all the people of the United States, but

107

in particular, with his grief-stricken wife and the other members of his family.

"During his recent visit here we came to regard the President as one of ourselves, though always aware that he was head of the greatest nation in the world today. We were proud of him as being one of our race and we were convinced that through his fearless leadership the United States could continue to increase its stature amongst the nations of the world and its power to maintain world peace.

"Our consolation is that he died in a noble cause and we pray that God will give to the United States another such leader."

Two days later Frank O'Connor wrote in the *Sunday Independent,* Dublin:

"John Fitzgerald Kennedy was a miracle. In three different ways he broke through age-old American prejudices against Catholics, against Irishmen and against intellectuals, and you have to have lived in America to realize how strong these prejudices are. Eleven years ago, in the bar of an exclusive Boston club, an old Bostonian said to me: 'Do you know, you're the first educated Irishman I've ever met?' At that time, the American universities themselves were being crippled by the McCarthy inquisition.

"Kennedy was the fine flower of that great university system. The American university took the Irish literary revival and put it fair and square on every arts course, and when we mock at young Americans who come here to study Yeats and Joyce, we are mocking at the very thing that straightened the backs of men like Kennedy, so that they no longer had to go around pretending they had a great-grandmother from Antrim and were really 'Scotch-Irish:'

"Kennedy treated the Scotch-Irish with the same good-natured contempt with which he treated the native Irish who were afraid of James Joyce's name, and he boldly spoke of Joyce in the Dail, where previously Joyce's name had never been heard except on some debate on evil literature.

"In his last speech in Texas he quoted brilliantly from a book of mine. He was not the man to be afraid of quoting some Irish writer, whom most of his audience had never heard of. He was leading the Irish in America out of a ghetto of humiliation and pretence and telling them that they were a people with a history and literature as good as the best. He was also leading educated Americans back into the field of Government from which they had been expelled by the distrust of intellectuals.

"On Thursday night I was called to the telephone to hear: 'President Kennedy is quoting from some book of yours in San Antonio, Texas'; on Friday night I was called to the telephone to hear: 'President Kennedy is dead.'

"I wept, partly for ourselves, who have lost a man that represented not only his own country but ours; partly for America, whose black fate struck it again."